This Nanny Log Book belongs to

_____

_____

Address:

Phone number:

e-mail:

Baby's informations

Baby's Name: **Birthday:**

Parents contact information		
Name		
Mobile phone		
Address		
e-mail		

Medical condition/ Allergies	Medicine	Supplies needed

Instruction from parents

_____
_____
_____
_____
_____

Daily Log

Date: Day:

M T W T F S S

Feeding

Time	Duration	Amount

Diapers

Time	Pee	Poo

Naps

Time	Duration

Mood

Baby's informations

Baby's Name: **Birthday:**

Parents contact information

Name		
Mobile phone		
Address		
e-mail		

Medical condition/ Allergies	Medicine	Supplies needed

Instruction from parents

_____

_____

_____

_____

_____

Daily Log

Date: **Day:**

M T W T F S S

Feeding

Time	Duration	Amount

Diapers

Time	Pee	Poo

Naps

Time	Duration

Mood

Baby's informations

Baby's Name: **Birthday:**

Parents contact information

Name		
Mobile phone		
Address		
e-mail		

Medical condition/ Allergies	Medicine	Supplies needed

Instruction from parents

_____
_____
_____
_____
_____

Daily Log

Date: Day:

                                        M T W T F S S

Feeding

Time	Duration	Amount

Diapers

Time	Pee	Poo

Naps

Time	Duration

Mood

Baby's informations

Baby's Name: **Birthday:**

Parents contact information

Name		
Mobile phone		
Address		
e-mail		

Medical condition/ Allergies	Medicine	Supplies needed

Instruction from parents

_____

_____

_____

_____

Daily Log

Date: **Day:**

                                                  M T W T F S S

Feeding

Time	Duration	Amount

Diapers

Time	Pee	Poo

Naps

Time	Duration

Mood

Baby's informations

Baby's Name: **Birthday:**

Parents contact information		
Name		
Mobile phone		
Address		
e-mail		

Medical condition/ Allergies	Medicine	Supplies needed

Instruction from parents

_____

_____

_____

_____

Daily Log

Date: Day:

M T W T F S S

Feeding

Time	Duration	Amount

Diapers

Time	Pee	Poo

Naps

Time	Duration

Mood

Baby's informations

Baby's Name: **Birthday:**

Parents contact information			
Name			
Mobile phone			
Address			
e-mail			

Medical condition/ Allergies	Medicine	Supplies needed

Instruction from parents

_____
_____
_____
_____
_____

Daily Log

Date: Day:

M T W T F S S

Feeding

Time	Duration	Amount

Diapers

Time	Pee	Poo

Naps

Time	Duration

Mood

Baby's informations

Baby's Name: **Birthday:**

Parents contact information			
Name			
Mobile phone			
Address			
e-mail			

Medical condition/ Allergies	Medicine	Supplies needed

Instruction from parents

_____

_____

_____

_____

_____

Daily Log

Date: Day:

M T W T F S S

Feeding

Time	Duration	Amount

Diapers

Time	Pee	Poo

Naps

Time	Duration

Mood

Baby's informations

Baby's Name: **Birthday:**

Parents contact information

Name		
Mobile phone		
Address		
e-mail		

Medical condition/ Allergies	Medicine	Supplies needed

Instruction from parents

_____

_____

_____

_____

_____

Daily Log

Date: Day:

　　　　　　　　　　　　　　　M T W T F S S

Feeding

Time	Duration	Amount

Diapers

Time	Pee	Poo

Naps

Time	Duration

Mood

Baby's informations

Baby's Name: Birthday:

Parents contact information		
Name		
Mobile phone		
Address		
e-mail		

Medical condition/ Allergies	Medicine	Supplies needed

Instruction from parents

_____
_____
_____
_____
_____

Daily Log

Date: Day:

                                    M T W T F S S

Feeding

Time	Duration	Amount

Diapers

Time	Pee	Poo

Naps

Time	Duration

Mood

Baby's informations

Baby's Name: **Birthday:**

Parents contact information		
Name		
Mobile phone		
Address		
e-mail		

Medical condition/ Allergies	Medicine	Supplies needed

Instruction from parents

_____

_____

_____

_____

Daily Log

Date: **Day:**

                                                                               M T W T F S S

Feeding

Time	Duration	Amount

Diapers

Time	Pee	Poo

Naps

Time	Duration

Mood

Baby's informations

Baby's Name: **Birthday:**

Parents contact information		
Name		
Mobile phone		
Address		
e-mail		

Medical condition/ Allergies	Medicine	Supplies needed

Instruction from parents

_____
_____
_____
_____

Daily Log

Date: Day:

M T W T F S S

Feeding

Time	Duration	Amount

Diapers

Time	Pee	Poo

Naps

Time	Duration

Mood

Baby's informations

Baby's Name: **Birthday:**

Parents contact information

Name		
Mobile phone		
Address		
e-mail		

Medical condition/ Allergies	Medicine	Supplies needed

Instruction from parents

_____
_____
_____
_____

Daily Log

Date: **Day:**

M T W T F S S

Feeding

Time	Duration	Amount

Diapers

Time	Pee	Poo

Naps

Time	Duration

Mood

Baby's informations

Baby's Name: **Birthday:**

Parents contact information			
Name			
Mobile phone			
Address			
e-mail			

Medical condition/ Allergies	Medicine	Supplies needed

Instruction from parents

_____
_____
_____
_____

Daily Log

Date: Day:

M T W T F S S

Feeding

Time	Duration	Amount

Diapers

Time	Pee	Poo

Naps

Time	Duration

Mood

Baby's informations

Baby's Name: **Birthday:**

Parents contact information		
Name		
Mobile phone		
Address		
e-mail		

Medical condition/ Allergies	Medicine	Supplies needed

Instruction from parents

_____

_____

_____

_____

Daily Log

Date: Day:
                                     M T W T F S S

Feeding

Time	Duration	Amount

Diapers

Time	Pee	Poo

Naps

Time	Duration

Mood

Baby's informations

Baby's Name: **Birthday:**

	Parents contact information	
Name		
Mobile phone		
Address		
e-mail		

Medical condition/ Allergies	Medicine	Supplies needed

Instruction from parents

_____

_____

_____

_____

Daily Log

Date: Day:

                                    M T W T F S S

Feeding

Time	Duration	Amount

Diapers

Time	Pee	Poo

Naps

Time	Duration

Mood

Baby's informations

Baby's Name: **Birthday:**

Parents contact information		
Name		
Mobile phone		
Address		
e-mail		

Medical condition/ Allergies	Medicine	Supplies needed

Instruction from parents

_____

_____

_____

_____

Daily Log

Date:　　　　　　　　　　　　　Day:

　　　　　　　　　　　　　　　M T W T F S S

Feeding

Time	Duration	Amount

Diapers

Time	Pee	Poo

Naps

Time	Duration

Mood

Baby's informations

Baby's Name: **Birthday:**

Parents contact information			
Name			
Mobile phone			
Address			
e-mail			

Medical condition/ Allergies	Medicine	Supplies needed

Instruction from parents

_____
_____
_____
_____

Daily Log

Date: Day:

M T W T F S S

Feeding

Time	Duration	Amount

Diapers

Time	Pee	Poo

Naps

Time	Duration

Mood

Baby's informations

Baby's Name: **Birthday:**

Parents contact information		
Name		
Mobile phone		
Address		
e-mail		

Medical condition/ Allergies	Medicine	Supplies needed

Instruction from parents

_____
_____
_____
_____
_____

Daily Log

Date: **Day:**

M T W T F S S

Feeding

Time	Duration	Amount

Diapers

Time	Pee	Poo

Naps

Time	Duration

Mood

Baby's informations

Baby's Name: **Birthday:**

Parents contact information			
Name			
Mobile phone			
Address			
e-mail			

Medical condition/ Allergies	Medicine	Supplies needed

Instruction from parents

_____
_____
_____
_____
_____

Daily Log

Date: **Day:**

M T W T F S S

Feeding

Time	Duration	Amount

Diapers

Time	Pee	Poo

Naps

Time	Duration

Mood

Baby's informations

Baby's Name: **Birthday:**

Parents contact information		
Name		
Mobile phone		
Address		
e-mail		

Medical condition/ Allergies	Medicine	Supplies needed

Instruction from parents

_____

_____

_____

_____

_____

Daily Log

Date: Day:

M T W T F S S

Feeding

Time	Duration	Amount

Diapers

Time	Pee	Poo

Naps

Time	Duration

Mood

Baby's informations

Baby's Name: **Birthday:**

Parents contact information		
Name		
Mobile phone		
Address		
e-mail		

Medical condition/ Allergies	Medicine	Supplies needed

Instruction from parents

_____
_____
_____
_____

Daily Log

Date: Day:

M T W T F S S

Feeding

Time	Duration	Amount

Diapers

Time	Pee	Poo

Naps

Time	Duration

Mood

Baby's informations

Baby's Name: **Birthday:**

Parents contact information		
Name		
Mobile phone		
Address		
e-mail		

Medical condition/ Allergies	Medicine	Supplies needed

Instruction from parents

_____

_____

_____

_____

Daily Log

Date: Day:

M T W T F S S

Feeding

Time	Duration	Amount

Diapers

Time	Pee	Poo

Naps

Time	Duration

Mood

Baby's informations

Baby's Name: **Birthday:**

Parents contact information			
Name			
Mobile phone			
Address			
e-mail			

Medical condition/ Allergies	Medicine	Supplies needed

Instruction from parents

_____
_____
_____
_____
_____

Daily Log

Date: Day:

M T W T F S S

Feeding

Time	Duration	Amount

Diapers

Time	Pee	Poo

Naps

Time	Duration

Mood

Baby's informations

Baby's Name: **Birthday:**

Parents contact information			
Name			
Mobile phone			
Address			
e-mail			

Medical condition/ Allergies	Medicine	Supplies needed

Instruction from parents

_____

_____

_____

_____

Daily Log

Date: Day:

M T W T F S S

Feeding

Time	Duration	Amount

Diapers

Time	Pee	Poo

Naps

Time	Duration

Mood

Baby's informations

Baby's Name: **Birthday:**

Parents contact information

Name		
Mobile phone		
Address		
e-mail		

Medical condition/ Allergies	Medicine	Supplies needed

Instruction from parents

_____
_____
_____
_____

Daily Log

Date: **Day:**

M T W T F S S

Feeding

Time	Duration	Amount

Diapers

Time	Pee	Poo

Naps

Time	Duration

Mood

Baby's informations

Baby's Name: **Birthday:**

Parents contact information		
Name		
Mobile phone		
Address		
e-mail		

Medical condition/ Allergies	Medicine	Supplies needed

Instruction from parents

_____

_____

_____

_____

Daily Log

Date: **Day:**

M T W T F S S

Feeding

Time	Duration	Amount

Diapers

Time	Pee	Poo

Naps

Time	Duration

Mood

Baby's informations

Baby's Name: **Birthday:**

Parents contact information			
Name			
Mobile phone			
Address			
e-mail			

Medical condition/ Allergies	Medicine	Supplies needed

Instruction from parents

_____
_____
_____
_____

Daily Log

Date: Day:

M T W T F S S

Feeding

Time	Duration	Amount

Diapers

Time	Pee	Poo

Naps

Time	Duration

Mood

Baby's informations

Baby's Name: **Birthday:**

Parents contact information			
Name			
Mobile phone			
Address			
e-mail			

Medical condition/ Allergies	Medicine	Supplies needed

Instruction from parents

_____

_____

_____

_____

Daily Log

Date: Day:

M T W T F S S

Feeding

Time	Duration	Amount

Diapers

Time	Pee	Poo

Naps

Time	Duration

Mood

Baby's informations

Baby's Name: **Birthday:**

Parents contact information			
Name			
Mobile phone			
Address			
e-mail			

Medical condition/ Allergies	Medicine	Supplies needed

Instruction from parents

_____
_____
_____
_____

Daily Log

Date: Day:

M T W T F S S

Feeding

Time	Duration	Amount

Diapers

Time	Pee	Poo

Naps

Time	Duration

Mood

Baby's informations

Baby's Name: **Birthday:**

Parents contact information			
Name			
Mobile phone			
Address			
e-mail			

Medical condition/ Allergies	Medicine	Supplies needed

Instruction from parents

_____

_____

_____

_____

Daily Log

Date: Day:

M T W T F S S

Feeding

Time	Duration	Amount

Diapers

Time	Pee	Poo

Naps

Time	Duration

Mood

Baby's informations

Baby's Name:　　　　　　　　　　**Birthday:**

Parents contact information

Name		
Mobile phone		
Address		
e-mail		

Medical condition/ Allergies	Medicine	Supplies needed

Instruction from parents

_____
_____
_____
_____

Daily Log

Date: Day:

M T W T F S S

Feeding

Time	Duration	Amount

Diapers

Time	Pee	Poo

Naps

Time	Duration

Mood

Baby's informations

Baby's Name: **Birthday:**

Parents contact information

Name		
Mobile phone		
Address		
e-mail		

Medical condition/ Allergies	Medicine	Supplies needed

Instruction from parents

_____
_____
_____
_____
_____

Daily Log

Date: **Day:**

M T W T F S S

Feeding

Time	Duration	Amount

Diapers

Time	Pee	Poo

Naps

Time	Duration

Mood

Baby's informations

Baby's Name: **Birthday:**

Parents contact information		
Name		
Mobile phone		
Address		
e-mail		

Medical condition/ Allergies	Medicine	Supplies needed

Instruction from parents

_____

_____

_____

_____

Daily Log

Date: Day:

M T W T F S S

Feeding

Time	Duration	Amount

Diapers

Time	Pee	Poo

Naps

Time	Duration

Mood

Baby's informations

Baby's Name: **Birthday:**

Parents contact information			
Name			
Mobile phone			
Address			
e-mail			

Medical condition/ Allergies	Medicine	Supplies needed

Instruction from parents

_____

_____

_____

_____

Daily Log

Date: Day:

                                         M T W T F S S

Feeding

Time	Duration	Amount

Diapers

Time	Pee	Poo

Naps

Time	Duration

Mood

Baby's informations

Baby's Name: **Birthday:**

Parents contact information			
Name			
Mobile phone			
Address			
e-mail			

Medical condition/ Allergies	Medicine	Supplies needed

Instruction from parents

_____

_____

_____

_____

Daily Log

Date: Day:

M T W T F S S

Feeding

Time	Duration	Amount

Diapers

Time	Pee	Poo

Naps

Time	Duration

Mood

Baby's informations

Baby's Name: **Birthday:**

Parents contact information		
Name		
Mobile phone		
Address		
e-mail		

Medical condition/ Allergies	Medicine	Supplies needed

Instruction from parents

_____

_____

_____

_____

_____

Daily Log

Date:

Day:

M T W T F S S

Feeding

Time	Duration	Amount

Diapers

Time	Pee	Poo

Naps

Time	Duration

Mood

Baby's informations

Baby's Name: **Birthday:**

Parents contact information

Name		
Mobile phone		
Address		
e-mail		

Medical condition/ Allergies	Medicine	Supplies needed

Instruction from parents

_____
_____
_____
_____

Daily Log

Date: Day:

MTWTFSS

Feeding

Time	Duration	Amount

Diapers

Time	Pee	Poo

Naps

Time	Duration

Mood

Baby's informations

Baby's Name: **Birthday:**

Parents contact information			
Name			
Mobile phone			
Address			
e-mail			

Medical condition/ Allergies	Medicine	Supplies needed

Instruction from parents

_____

_____

_____

_____

_____

Daily Log

Date: **Day:**

M   T   W   T   F   S   S

Feeding

Time	Duration	Amount

Diapers

Time	Pee	Poo

Naps

Time	Duration

Mood

Baby's informations

Baby's Name: **Birthday:**

Parents contact information		
Name		
Mobile phone		
Address		
e-mail		

Medical condition/ Allergies	Medicine	Supplies needed

Instruction from parents

_____
_____
_____
_____

Daily Log

Date: **Day:**

M T W T F S S

Feeding

Time	Duration	Amount

Diapers

Time	Pee	Poo

Naps

Time	Duration

Mood

Baby's informations

Baby's Name: **Birthday:**

Parents contact information		
Name		
Mobile phone		
Address		
e-mail		

Medical condition/ Allergies	Medicine	Supplies needed

Instruction from parents

_____

_____

_____

_____

Daily Log

Date: **Day:**

M T W T F S S

Feeding

Time	Duration	Amount

Diapers

Time	Pee	Poo

Naps

Time	Duration

Mood

Baby's informations

Baby's Name: **Birthday:**

Parents contact information		
Name		
Mobile phone		
Address		
e-mail		

Medical condition/ Allergies	Medicine	Supplies needed

Instruction from parents

_____
_____
_____
_____

Daily Log

Date: **Day:**

                                                 M T W T F S S

Feeding

Time	Duration	Amount

Diapers

Time	Pee	Poo

Naps

Time	Duration

Mood

Baby's informations

Baby's Name: **Birthday:**

Parents contact information

Name		
Mobile phone		
Address		
e-mail		

Medical condition/ Allergies	Medicine	Supplies needed

Instruction from parents

_____

_____

_____

_____

_____

Daily Log

Date: Day:

M T W T F S S

Feeding

Time	Duration	Amount

Diapers

Time	Pee	Poo

Naps

Time	Duration

Mood

Baby's informations

Baby's Name: **Birthday:**

Parents contact information

Name		
Mobile phone		
Address		
e-mail		

Medical condition/ Allergies	Medicine	Supplies needed

Instruction from parents

_____

_____

_____

_____

_____

Daily Log

Date: Day:

M T W T F S S

Feeding

Time	Duration	Amount

Diapers

Time	Pee	Poo

Naps

Time	Duration

Mood

Baby's informations

Baby's Name: **Birthday:**

Parents contact information

Name		
Mobile phone		
Address		
e-mail		

Medical condition/ Allergies	Medicine	Supplies needed

Instruction from parents

_____

_____

_____

_____

_____

Daily Log

Date:

Day:

M T W T F S S

Feeding

Time	Duration	Amount

Diapers

Time	Pee	Poo

Naps

Time	Duration

Mood

Baby's informations

Baby's Name: **Birthday:**

Parents contact information		
Name		
Mobile phone		
Address		
e-mail		

Medical condition/ Allergies	Medicine	Supplies needed

Instruction from parents

_____
_____
_____
_____

Daily Log

Date: **Day:**

M T W T F S S

Feeding

Time	Duration	Amount

Diapers

Time	Pee	Poo

Naps

Time	Duration

Mood

Baby's informations

Baby's Name: **Birthday:**

Parents contact information		
Name		
Mobile phone		
Address		
e-mail		

Medical condition/ Allergies	Medicine	Supplies needed

Instruction from parents

_____

_____

_____

_____

Daily Log

Date: Day:

M T W T F S S

Feeding

Time	Duration	Amount

Diapers

Time	Pee	Poo

Naps

Time	Duration

Mood

Baby's informations

Baby's Name:　　　　　　　　**Birthday:**

Parents contact information		
Name		
Mobile phone		
Address		
e-mail		

Medical condition/ Allergies	Medicine	Supplies needed

Instruction from parents

_____
_____
_____
_____
_____

Daily Log

Date: Day:

M T W T F S S

Feeding

Time	Duration	Amount

Diapers

Time	Pee	Poo

Naps

Time	Duration

Mood

Baby's informations

Baby's Name: **Birthday:**

Parents contact information			
Name			
Mobile phone			
Address			
e-mail			

Medical condition/ Allergies	Medicine	Supplies needed

Instruction from parents

_____

_____

_____

_____

Daily Log

Date: Day:

M T W T F S S

Feeding

Time	Duration	Amount

Diapers

Time	Pee	Poo

Naps

Time	Duration

Mood

Baby's informations

Baby's Name: **Birthday:**

Parents contact information			
Name			
Mobile phone			
Address			
e-mail			

Medical condition/ Allergies	Medicine	Supplies needed

Instruction from parents

_____
_____
_____
_____
_____

Daily Log

Date: **Day:**

M T W T F S S

Feeding

Time	Duration	Amount

Diapers

Time	Pee	Poo

Naps

Time	Duration

Mood

www.ingramcontent.com/pod-product-compliance
Lightning Source LLC
LaVergne TN
LVHW060212080526
838202LV00052B/4258